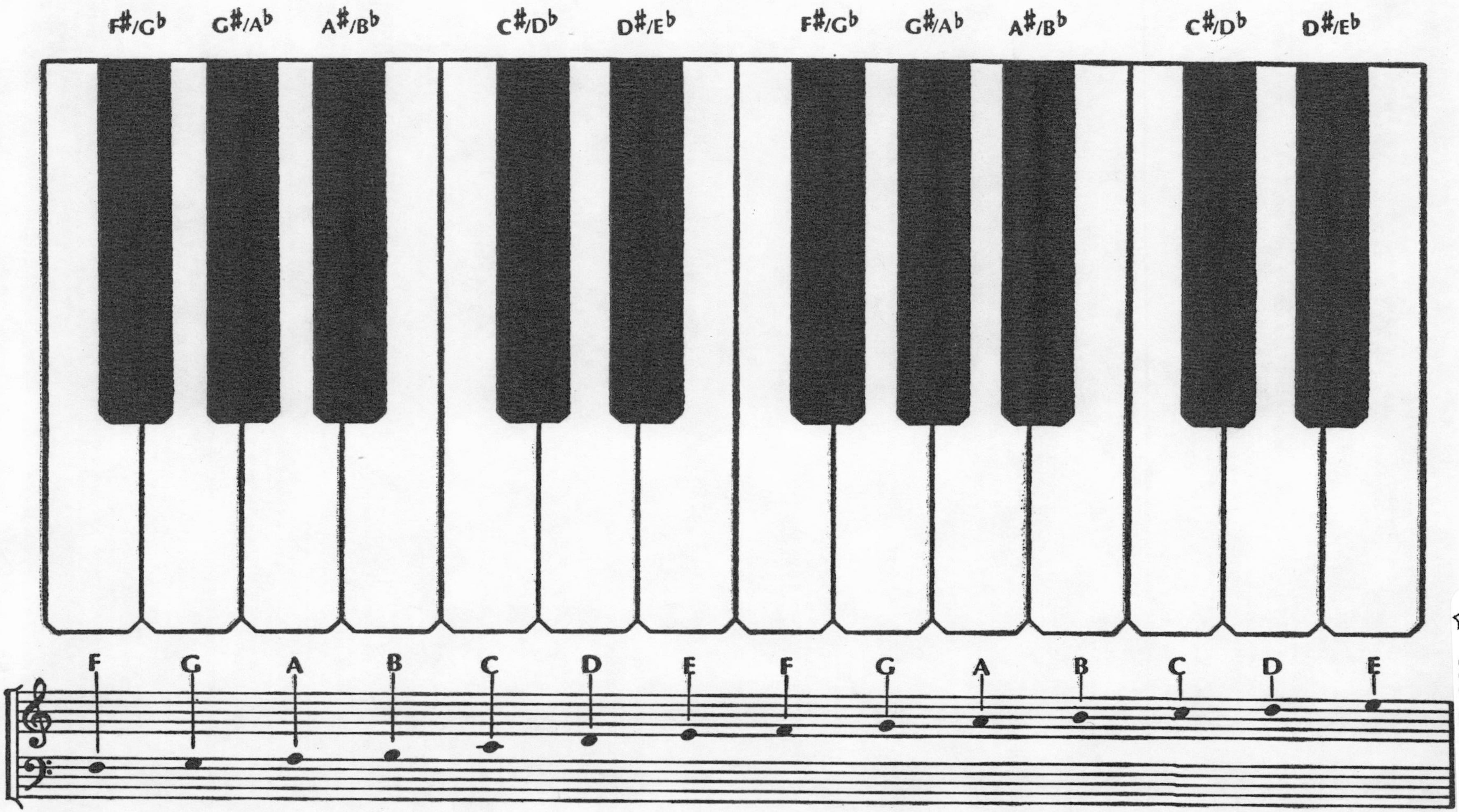

F♯/G♭ G♯/A♭ A♯/B♭ C♯/D♭ D♯/E♭ F♯/G♭ G♯/A♭ A♯/B♭ C♯/D♭ D♯/E♭

F G A B C D E F G A B C D E

World of Music

Mary Palmer • Mary Louise Reilly
Carol Rogel Scott
Authors

Carmino Ravosa • Phyllis Weikart
Theme Musical — Movement

Darrell Bledsoe
Producer, Vocal Recordings

Silver Burdett & Ginn
Morristown, NJ • Needham, MA
Atlanta, GA • Cincinnati, OH • Dallas, TX • Menlo Park, CA • Deerfield, IL

ISBN 0-382-07044-5

Contents

Music for Living 2

Five Kites 4
Hush! 5
Jimbo's Lullaby 6
A Singing Game 8
A Game Song 9
Work Sounds 10
Here Comes the Band! 12
The Seasons 14
It Rained a Mist 16
A Story Song 18
Departure 20
The Little Green Frog 22
Fiddle-dee-dee 23

Understanding Music 24

Sounds 26
Percussion Sounds 28
Listen! 30
Keeping the Beat 32
A Game Song 33
Long and Short 34
A Singing Game 35
Long Sounds, Short Sounds 36
Impromptu—The Top 38
Phrases 40
High and Low 42
High and Low Sounds 44
Repeated Tones 46
At the Park 48
Upward and Downward 50
Andante 52
Fine Arts 54
Finding a Pattern 55

Sharing Music 56

Moving and Playing 58
Playing a Pattern 60
A Marching Song 62
Marche Militaire 64
Sounds of Instruments 66
A Nonsense Song 68
An Action Song 70
One More River 71
Playing Bells 72
Playing Instruments 73
A Traditional Song 74
Rhythm-Pattern Detectives 76
Playing Bells 77
An Action Song 78
Gavotte 80

THEME MUSICAL 82
One Big Happy Family

Sing and Celebrate 84

Sounds of Halloween 86
I Know a Secret 87

Reference Bank

Can You Read This? 88
Sound Bank 80
Glossary 92
Classified Index 93
Song Index 94
Picture Credits 94

FIVE & DIME
HARDWARE

MUSIC FOR LIVING

·TACO·
MILK

Five Kites

You can sing the kites off into the sky.
Play the bells with your singing.

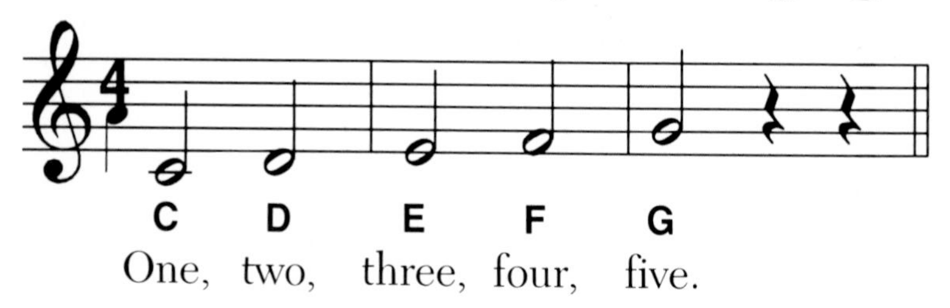
C D E F G
One, two, three, four, five.

Hush!

Look at the painting.
Use your own words to tell what you see.

WINTER EVENING
JEAN FRANCOIS MILLET

Jimbo's Lullaby

Time for bed, Jimbo!

LISTENING
1
SKILLS

"Jimbo's Lullaby" from <u>Children's Corner Suite</u> .... Debussy

1.
2.
3.

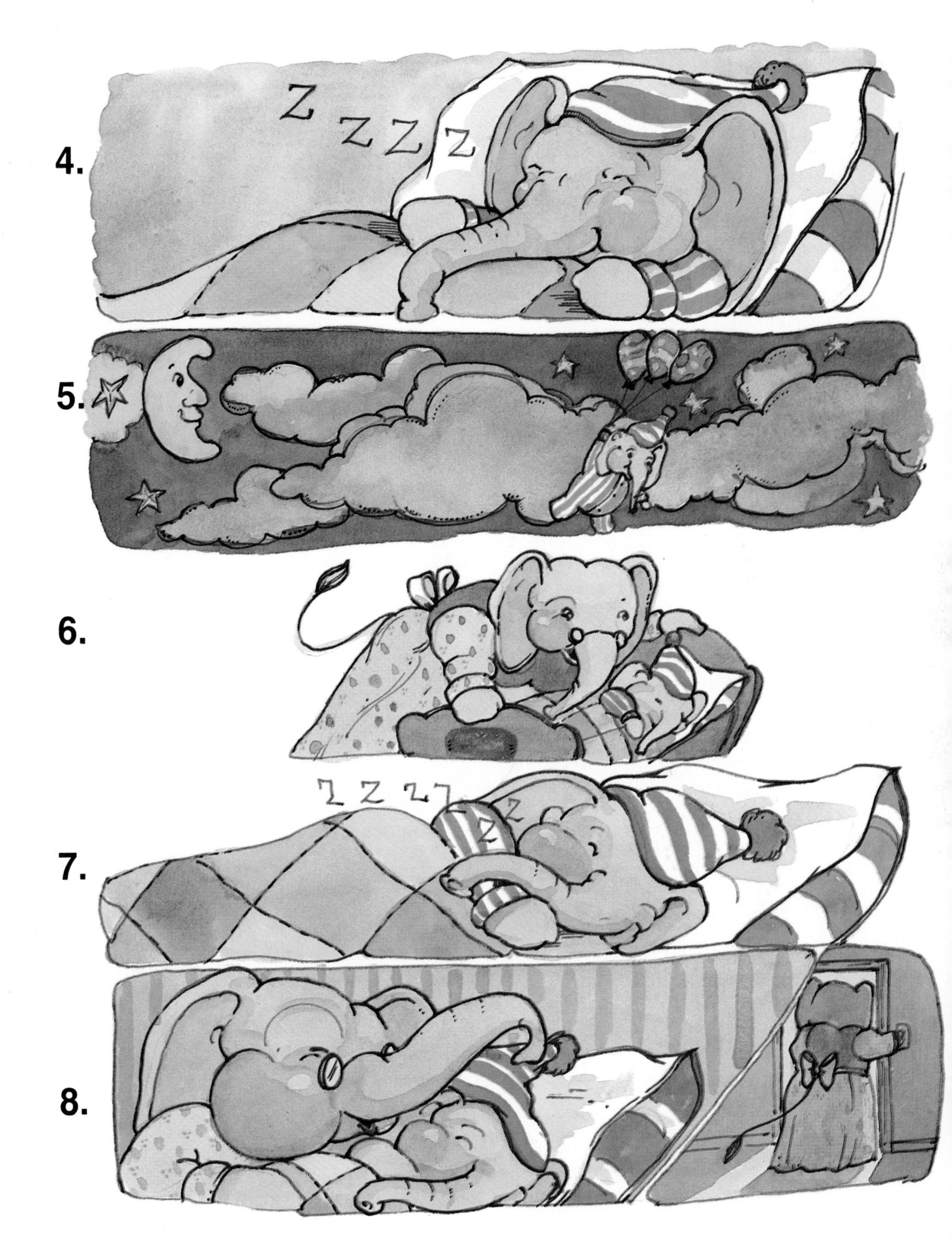
4.
5.
6.
7.
8.

A Singing Game

Here is a chant that you can sing.
Pat the rhythm of the repeated words.

Miss Mary Mack
Singing Game
Miss Mary Mack, Mack, Mack,
All dressed in black, black, black,
With silver but-tons, but-tons, but-tons
Down her back, back, back;
She asked her moth-er, moth-er, moth-er
For fifty cents, cents, cents,
To see the el-e-phant, el-e-phant, el-e-phant
Jump the fence, fence, fence.

A Game Song

Have you ever played a game all day long?

Listen for all

day

long in this song.

Come on Through, Miss Sally

American Folk Game

VERSE:

2 This the way we pull away,

All day long.

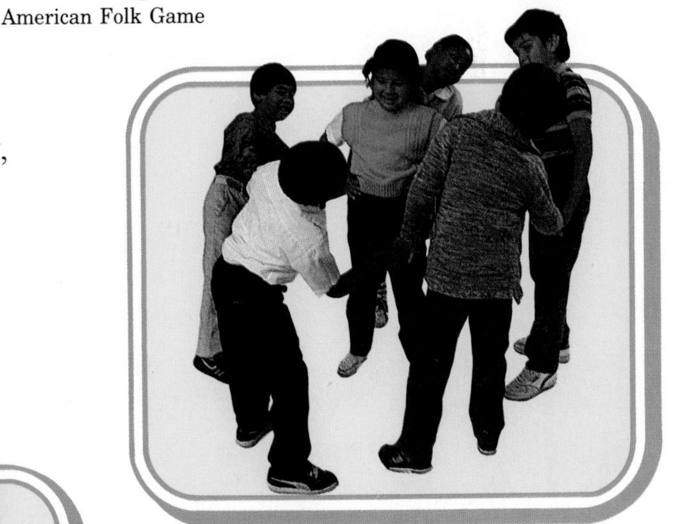

REFRAIN:

Come on through, Miss Sally,

All day long.

Work Sounds

What is happening in these pictures?

Imagine that you are watching
the workers.

What sounds would you hear?

Tear it down!

Build it up!

Here Comes the Band!

Which band instrument do you like best?
Pretend to play it with the recording.

I Like a Band

Words and Music by Samuel Drake

1. The band starts to play, far a - way down the street,

And I hum the tune, keep-ing time with my feet.

I stand by the curb, and I cheer when they come.

I do like the sound of a big bass drum!

2. The drum major leads, and he
   twirls his baton,
   He looks very fine as he comes
   marching on.
   They play very loud, and they
   sound very grand.
   I do like the sound of a
   big brass band!

The Seasons

Which picture shows a summer scene?

Which seasons do the other pictures show?

Here is a song about the seasons.

The curved lines show the phrases
in the melody.

How many phrases are there?
Try to sing each phrase in one breath.

The Seasons

Folk Song from Germany

1. Oh, there are four sea-sons that make up the year,

And I'll tell you how I know which sea-son's here.

2. The springtime brings flowers for
   pretty bouquets;
   In summer we have lots of warm,
   sunny days.

3. The autumn brings harvests of
   good things to eat;
   In winter there's ice and snow
   under my feet.

It Rained a Mist

The houses show how the melody begins.

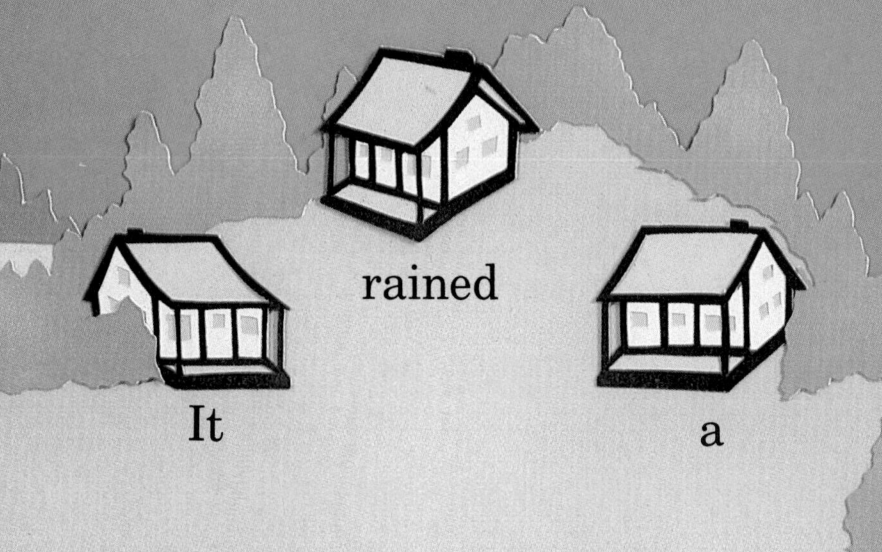
It
rained
a

mist,

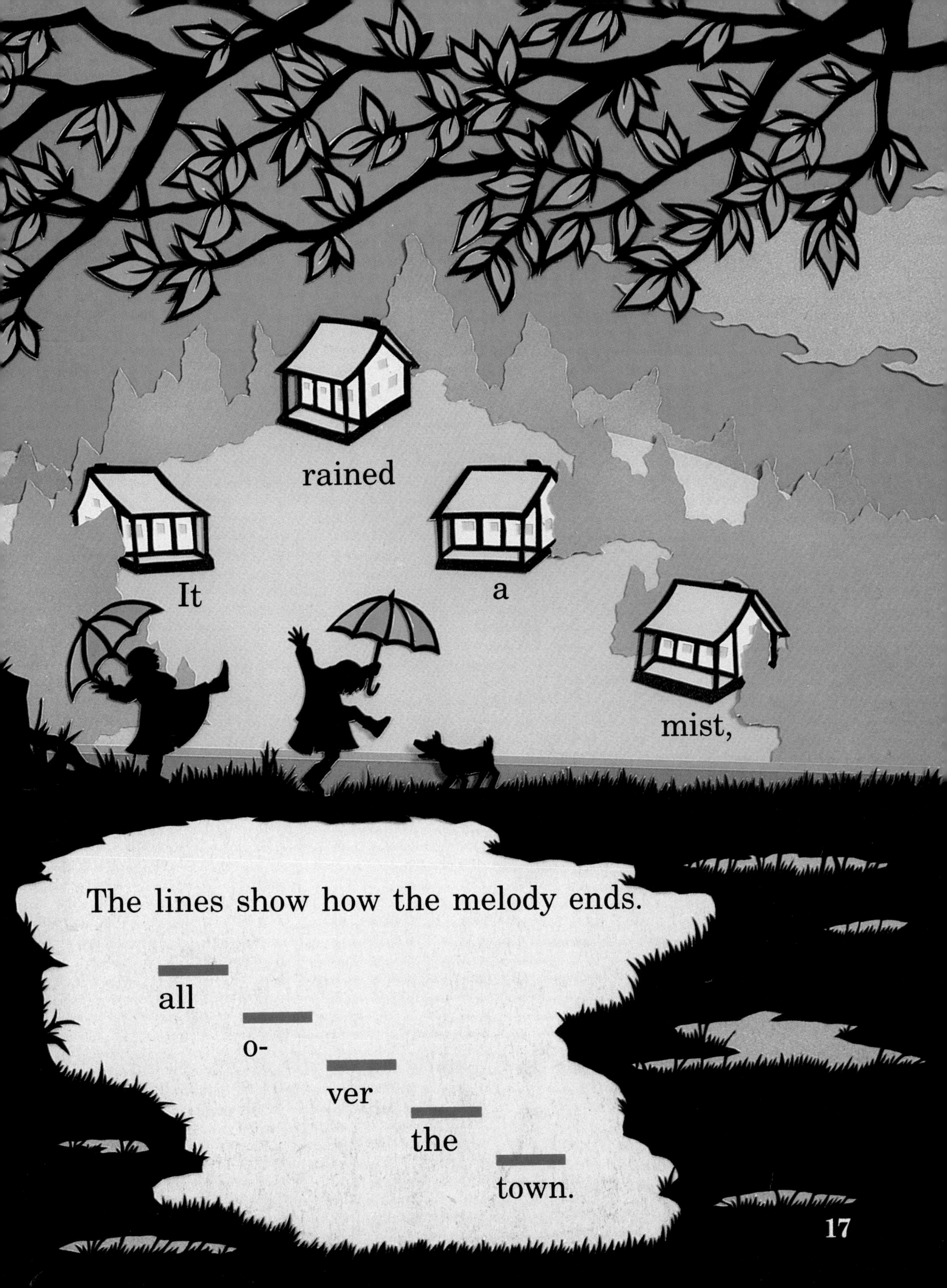
rained
It
a
mist,
The lines show how the melody ends.
all
o-
ver
the
town.

A Story Song

Listen for the story that this song tells.

When you are ready, act it out.

The Snowman

Folk Song from Canada

1. Once a jol - ly snow - man stood out - side the door,

Thought he'd like to come in - side and play up - on the floor,

Thought he'd like to warm him-self, By the fire-light red,

Thought he'd like to climb up - on the big white bed.

2. So he called the north wind:
"Help me, wind, I pray,
I'm completely frozen standing
here all day."
So the north wind came along,
Blew him in the door,
Now there's nothing left of him
but a puddle on the floor.

Departure

All aboard!

LISTENING SKILLS 2 "Departure" from Winter Bonfire . . . . Prokofiev

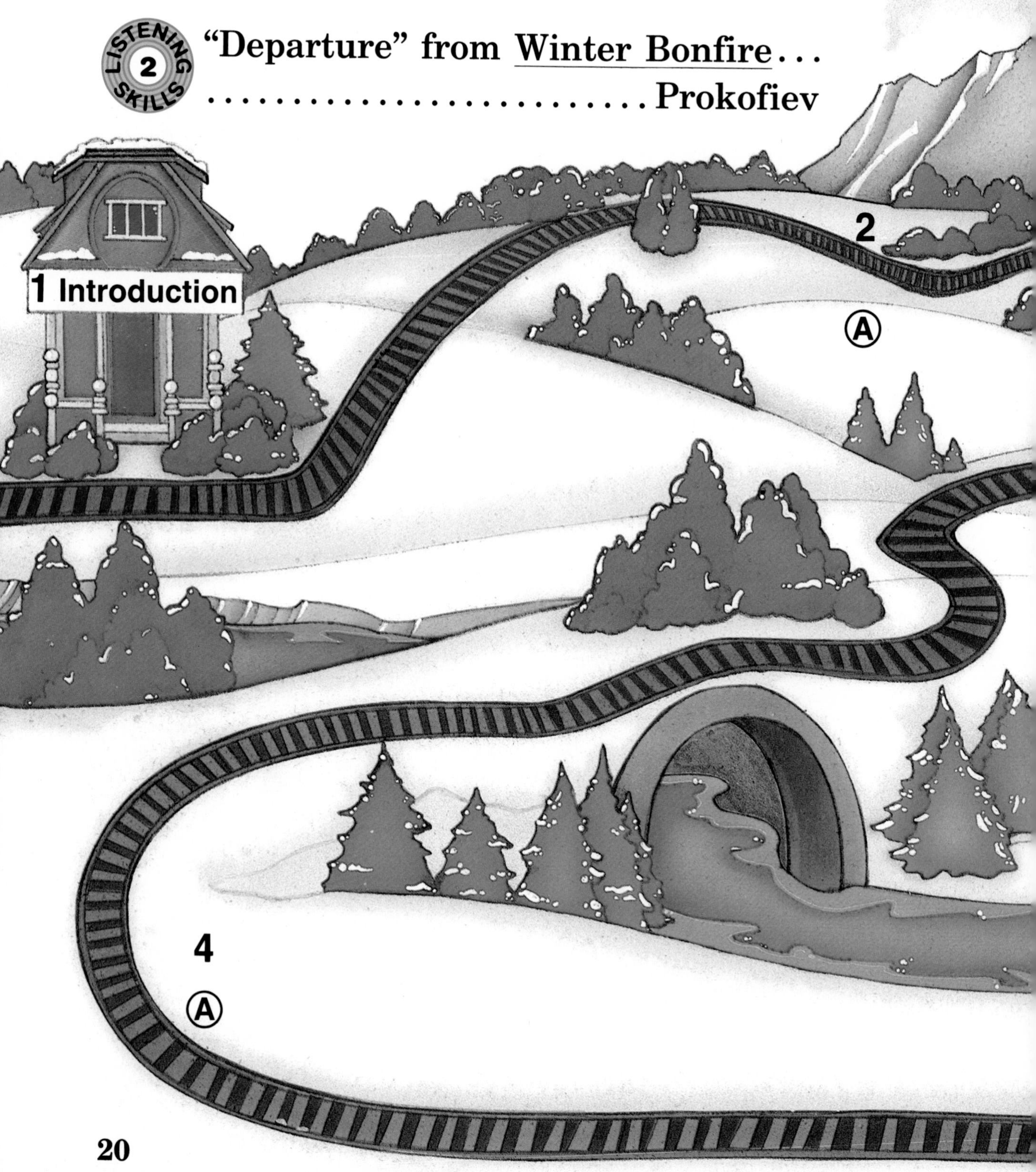

1 Introduction
2
A
4
A

3
B
5 Ending

The Little Green Frog
Traditional
lump!
Ga-
C F
Ga - lump! went the little green frog one day,
C F
Ga - lump! went the little green frog;
C F
Ga - lump! went the little green frog one day,
C F
And his eyes went ga - lump!

Fiddle-dee-dee

Lines can show the sound.

F♯ D D D

Fid - dle - dee - dee

Notes also show the sound.

F♯ D

Fid - dle - dee - dee

high
Cock-a-Doodle DOO!!
Tweet Tweet
soft
loud
steady beat
low
same
different

UNDERSTANDING MUSIC

upward
downward
long
short
slow
fast

Sounds

We hear sounds in the city.

We hear sounds in the country.

Percussion Sounds

Each instrument has its own look.
Each instrument has its own sound.

cymbals

snare
drum

gourd
rattle

bass
xylophone

glockenspiel

guiro

maracas

conga drum

Listen!

Some sounds have a steady beat.

ALFRED WILLIAM
STATE
OF

Other sounds have no beat.

WESTERN SALISBURY
FIRE CO.
MACK

Keeping the Beat

Keep a steady beat as you chant this rhyme.

Bounce High, Bounce Low

Traditional

Bounce high,
Bounce low,
Bounce the ball to
Shi - loh.

A Game Song

Children in Africa play this singing game.

Obwisana

Folk Song from Ghana

Ob - wi - sa - na sa - na - na Ob - wi - sa - na sa.

Ob - wi - sa - na sa - na - na Ob - wi - sa - na sa.

Long and Short

Balloon Path

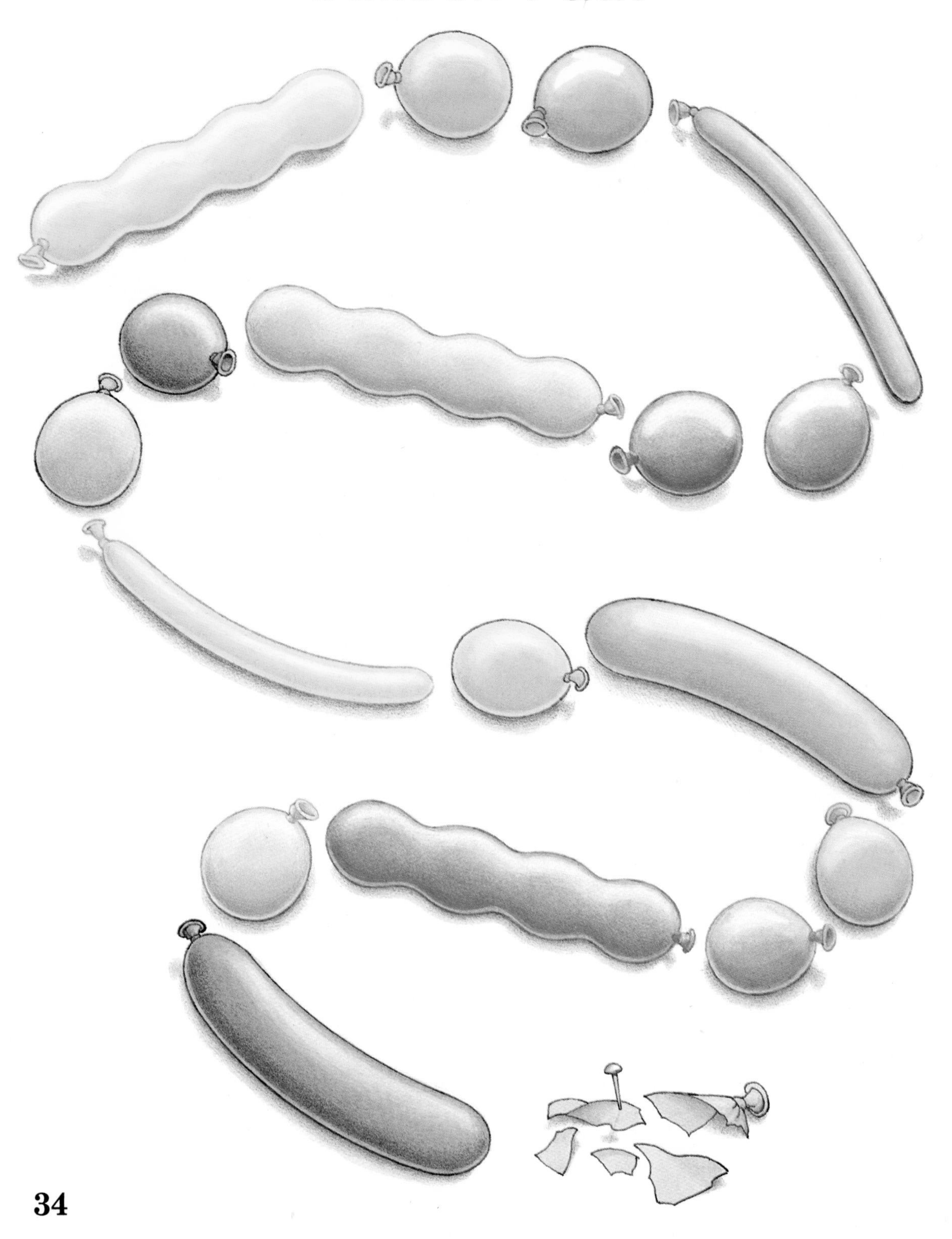

A Singing Game

Button, You Must Wander

Game Song

But - ton, you must wan - der, wan - der, wan - der,

F
But - ton, you must wan - der ev - 'ry - where.

Bright eyes will find you, sharp eyes will find you.

F
But - ton, you must wan - der ev - 'ry - where.

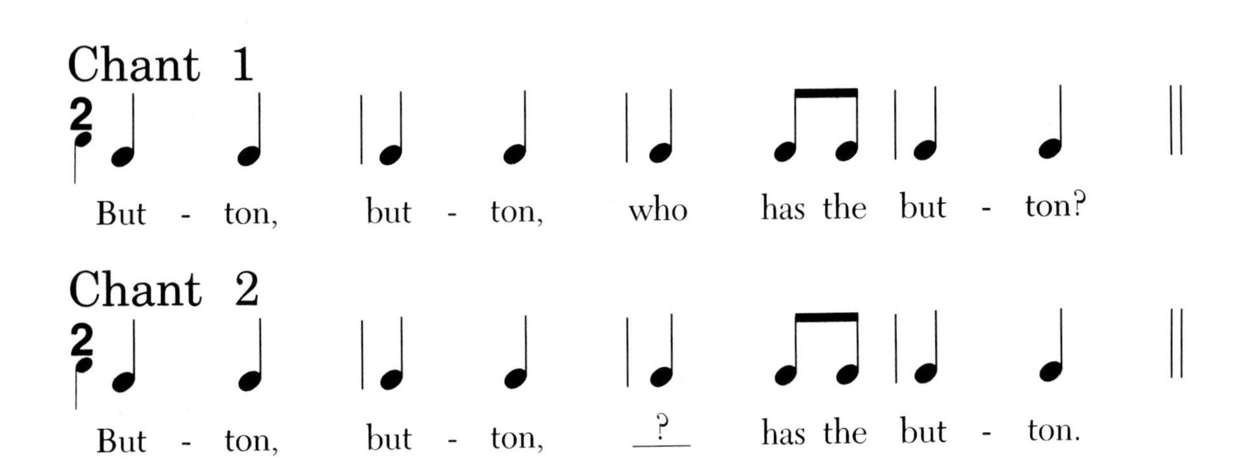
Chant 1
But - ton, but - ton, who has the but - ton?
Chant 2
But - ton, but - ton, ? has the but - ton.

Long Sounds, Short Sounds

This song has a part that is spoken.
Are the spoken sounds long or short?

Arre, caballito
3
Folk Song from Spain
English Words by Verne Muñoz
1. ¡A - rre, ca - ba - lli - to!
Hur - ry through the gate;
There's a cel - e - bra - tion,

And we will be late.
¡A - rre, a - rre, a - rre!
For we will be late.

2. ¡Arre, caballito!
There's no time to wait;
Tomorrow's the fiesta,
And we will be late.
¡Arre, arre, arre!
For we will be late.

Which pattern has short sounds?

1.

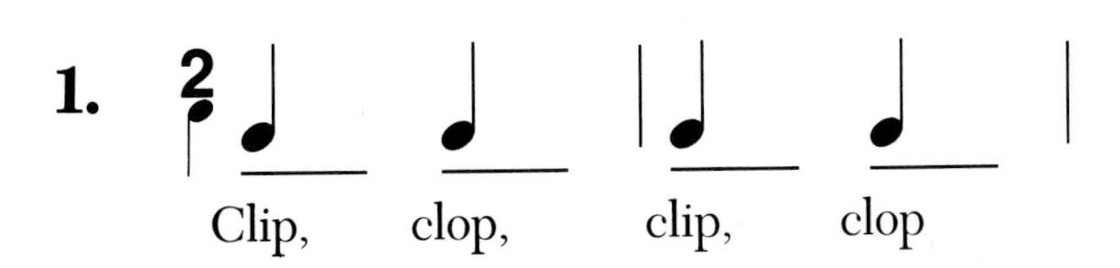
2
Clip, clop, clip, clop

2. 2

A - rre, a - rre, a - rre, a - rre

Impromptu—The Top

These pictures tell the story of a top.

Listen to the music to learn how the story ends.

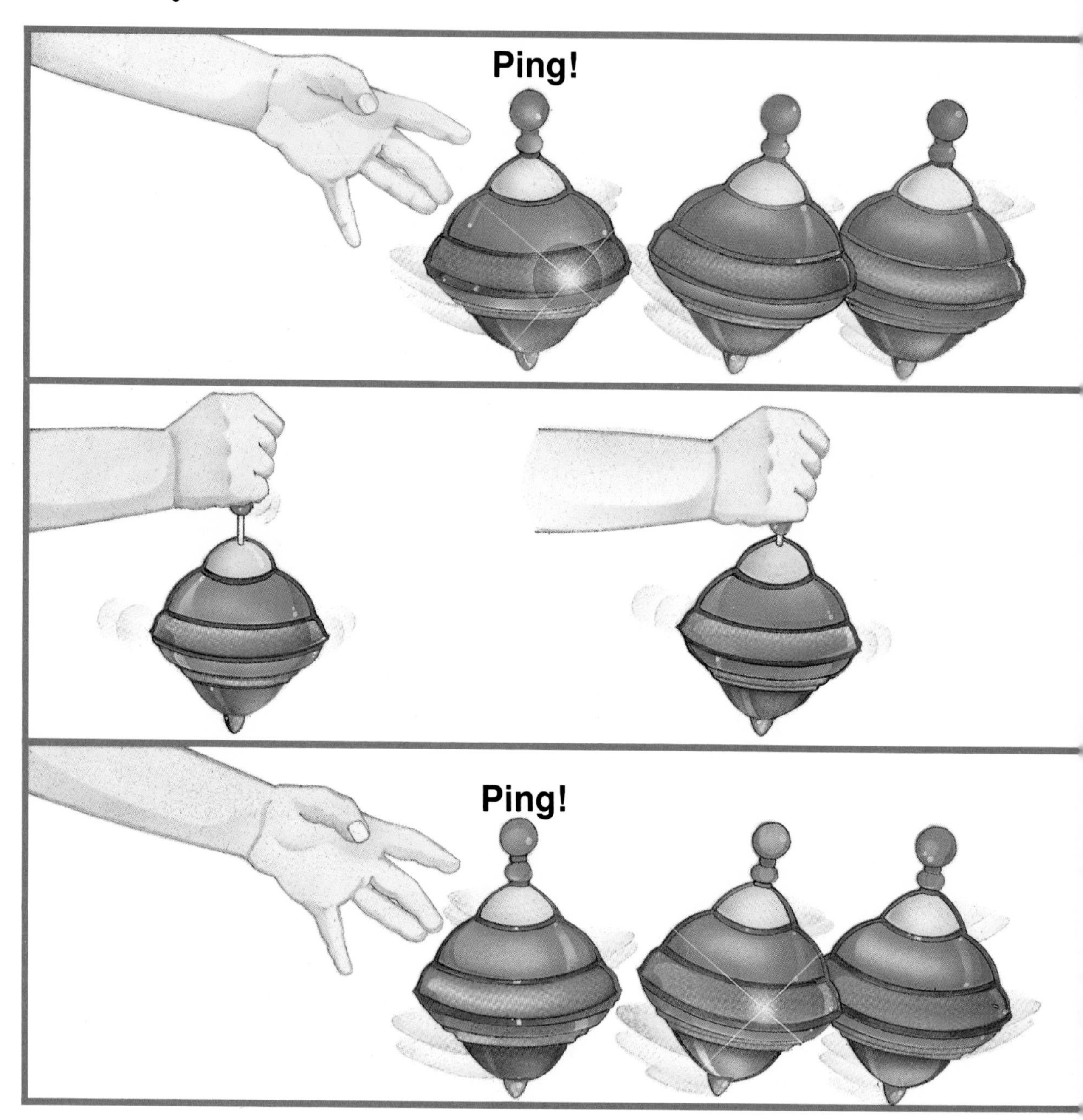
Ping!
Ping!

LISTENING
3
SKILLS

"Impromptu—The Top" from Children's Games . . . . . . Bizet

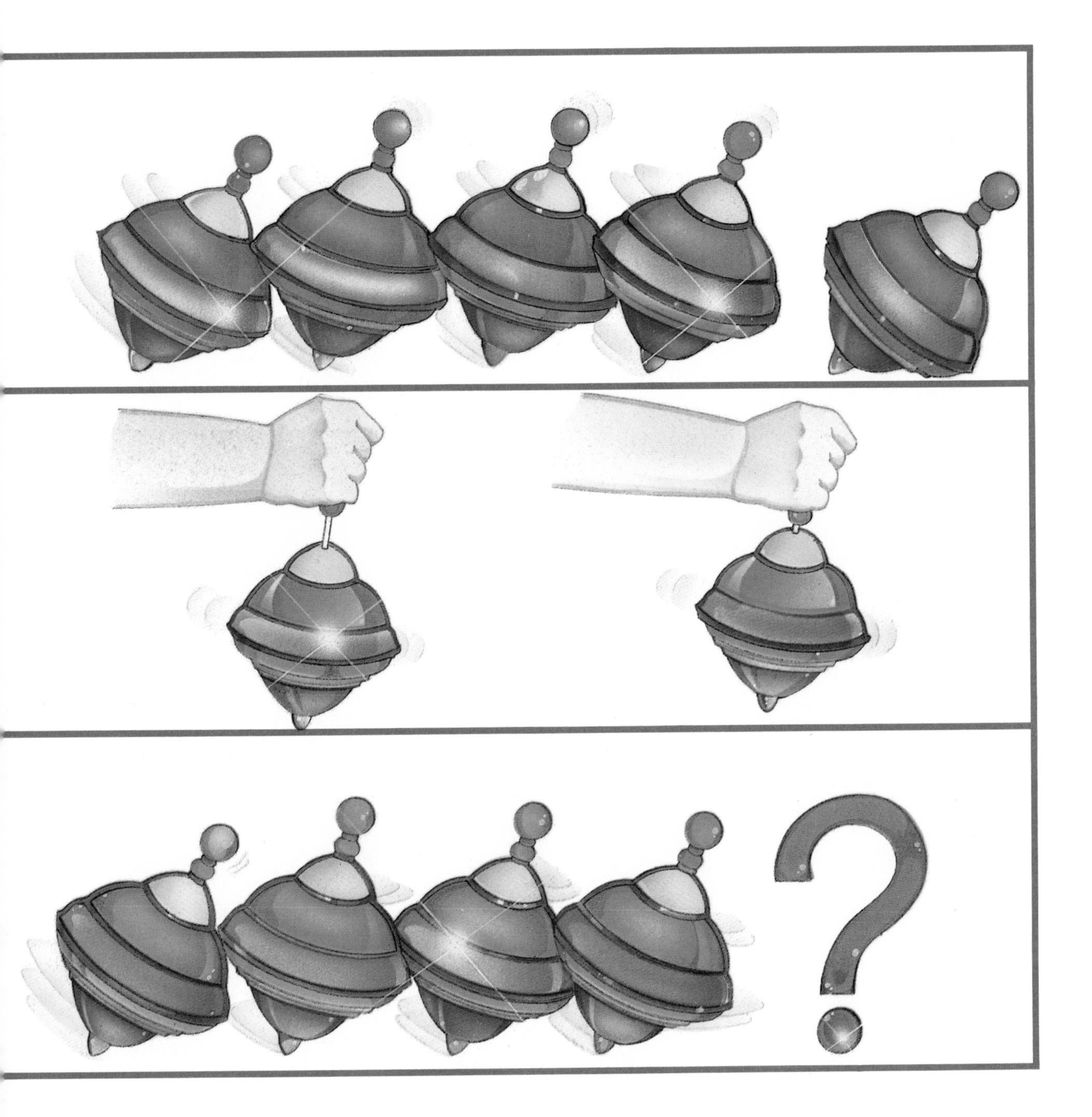

Phrases

THE LITTLE LAKE
JOSEPH STELLA

Find the phrases in this song.

Ay-lye, lyu-lye
3
Yiddish Folk Song
English Words by Richard Morris
1. Ay - lye, lyu - lye, lyu - lye,
Go to sleep now, don't cry;
Close your eyes in slum - ber,
Oh, my dar - ling kind' - lach.

2. Very soon I'll wake you,
To the fair I'll take you;
There'll be joy and laughter,
Oh, my darling kind'lach.

3. You will find such treats there,
Such good things to eat there;
Rolls with apple butter,
Oh, my darling kind'lach.

4. Ay-lye, lyu-lye, lyu-lye,
Go to sleep now, don't cry;
Close your eyes in slumber,
Oh, my darling kind'lach.

High and Low

High and Low Sounds

Look at the notes in the color boxes.

Where do you see notes that leap from high to low?

Bye'm Bye

Folk Song from Texas

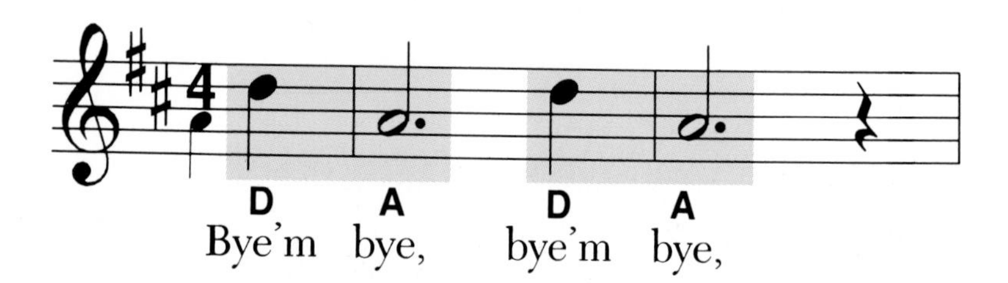
D A D A
Bye'm bye, bye'm bye,

A
Stars shin - ing,

Number, number one,

number two,

number three,

number four,

number five,

D D
Oh, my!

Bye'm bye, bye'm bye,

D D
Oh, my!

Bye'm bye.

Play the sound of <u>bye'm bye</u> on bells.

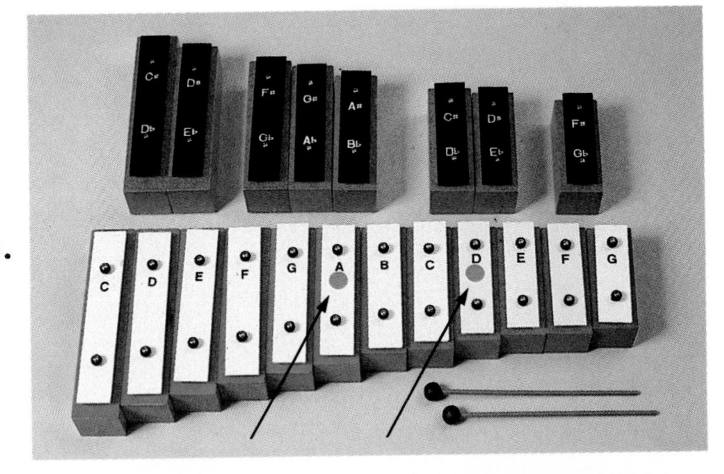
C D E F G A B C D E F G

Play the sound of <u>Oh, my!</u>

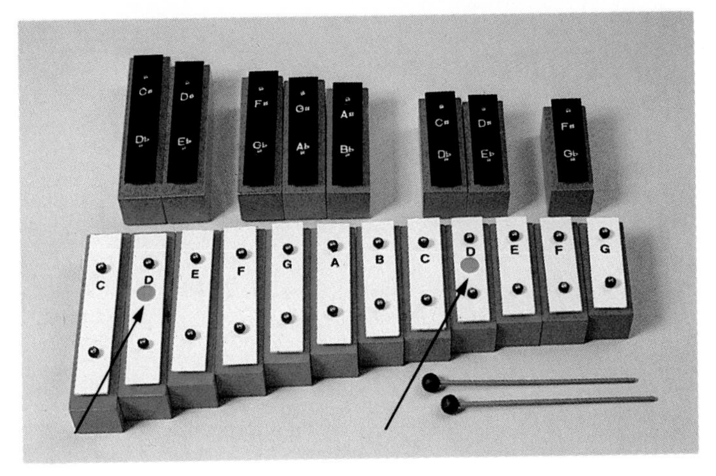
C D E F G A B C D E F G

Repeated Tones

Sing and play the repeated tones.

John the Rabbit

American Folk Game Song

E

Old John the rabbit, Oh, yes!

Old John the rabbit, Oh, yes!

Got a mighty bad habit, Oh, yes!

Of going to my garden, Oh, yes!

And eating up my peas, Oh, yes!

And cutting down my cabbage, Oh, yes!

He ate tomatoes,

Oh, yes!

And sweet potatoes,

Oh, yes!

And if I live,

Oh, yes!

To see next fall,

Oh, yes!

I won't have,

Oh, yes!

A garden at all!

At the Park

Where are the children moving upward? Downward?

Upward and Downward

Find sounds that move upward.
Find sounds that move downward.

Ebeneezer Sneezer

Words and Music by Lynn Freeman Olson

4
C

Ebeneezer Sneezer,

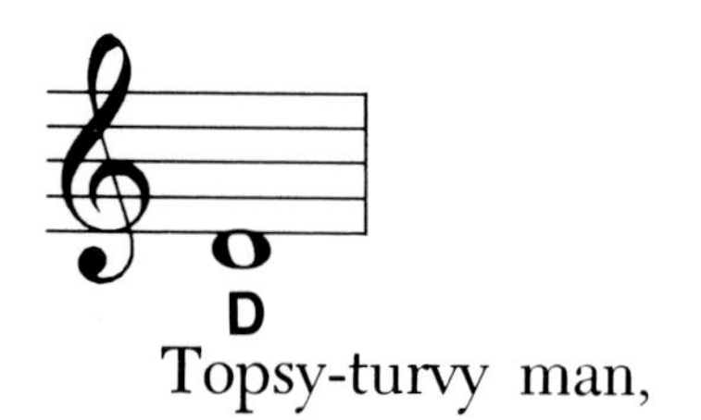
D

Topsy-turvy man,

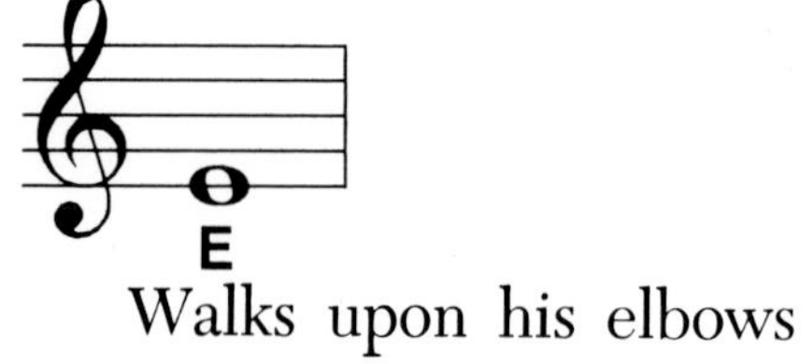
E

Walks upon his elbows

F

Ev'ry time he can,

G
Dresses up in paper
A
Ev'ry time it pours,
B
Whistles "Yankee Doodle"
C
Ev'ry time he snores.
Oh, E - be - nee - zer, what a man!

Andante

Listen for the surprise in this music.

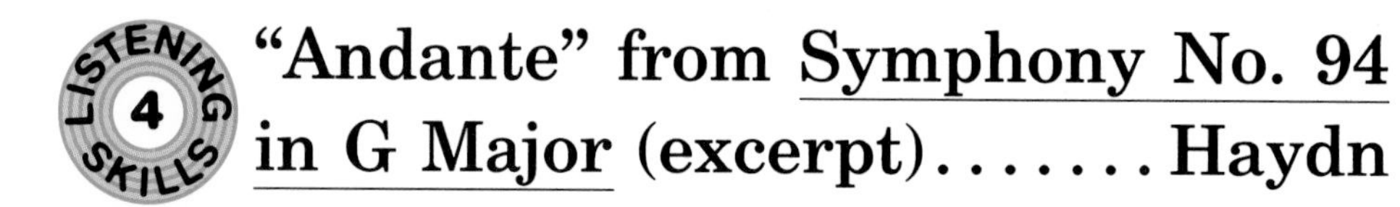

LISTENING
4
SKILLS

"Andante" from Symphony No. 94 in G Major (excerpt)........Haydn

Follow these notes as you listen.

4

Fine Arts

Look at this painting.
Do you see things that repeat?

BILL
CARLO
No. 5
ART Co
C. D.
W. C. W.

I SAW THE FIGURE 5 IN GOLD
CHARLES DEMUTH

Finding a Pattern

Look for this pattern in the music below.

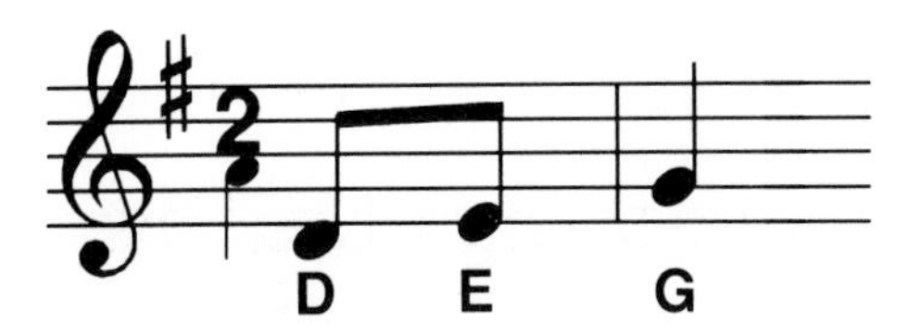
D E G

How many times do you see it?

The Angel Band

Folk Song from South Carolina

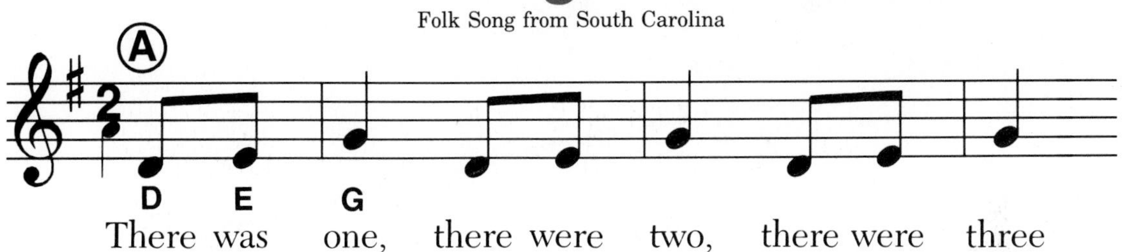
A
D E G
There was one, there were two, there were three

little angels,

D E G
There were four, there were five, there were six

little angels,

D E G
There were seven, there were eight, there were nine

little angels,

Ten little angels in that band.

BIG
SHOW
TODAY
TICKETS
5¢

Sharing Music

B·I·N·GO

Moving and Playing

Tell the story of this song without words.

Use short movements.

Use long movements.

4
Grinding Corn

Hopi Indian Song

Grind - ing corn, grind - ing corn,

In - dian maid - ens grind - ing corn;

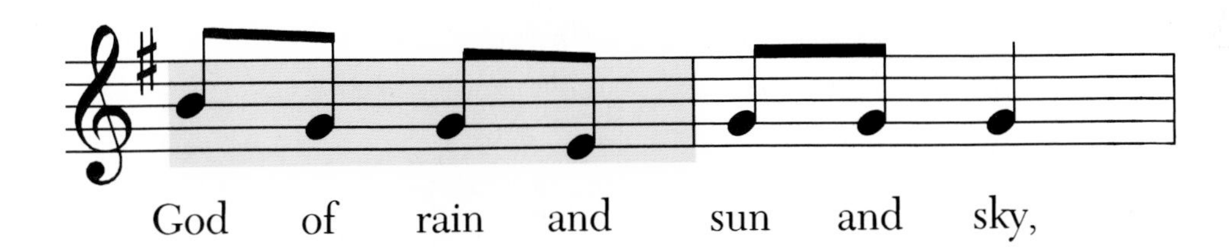
God of rain and sun and sky,

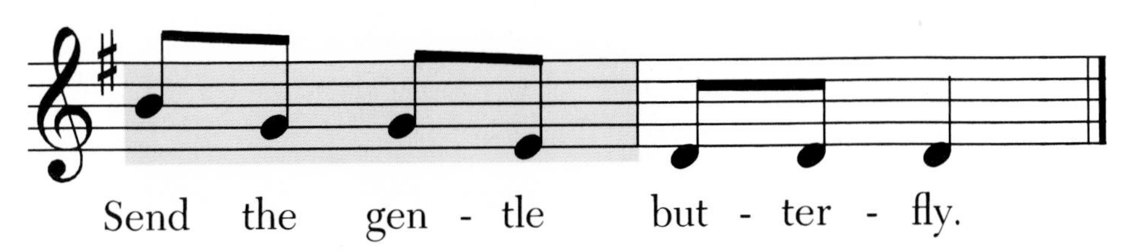
Send the gen - tle but - ter - fly.

Add instruments to the song.

Play short sounds.

maracas

Play the steady beat.

tom-tom

Play long sounds.

guiro

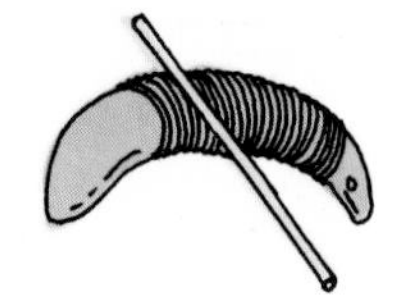

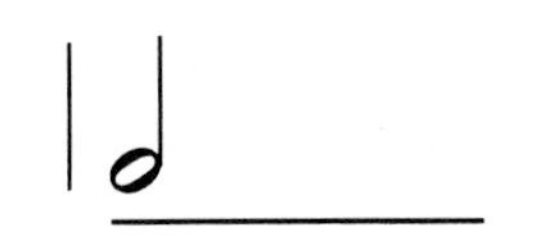

Playing a Pattern

You can play a pattern on instruments.
Which instrument will you play?

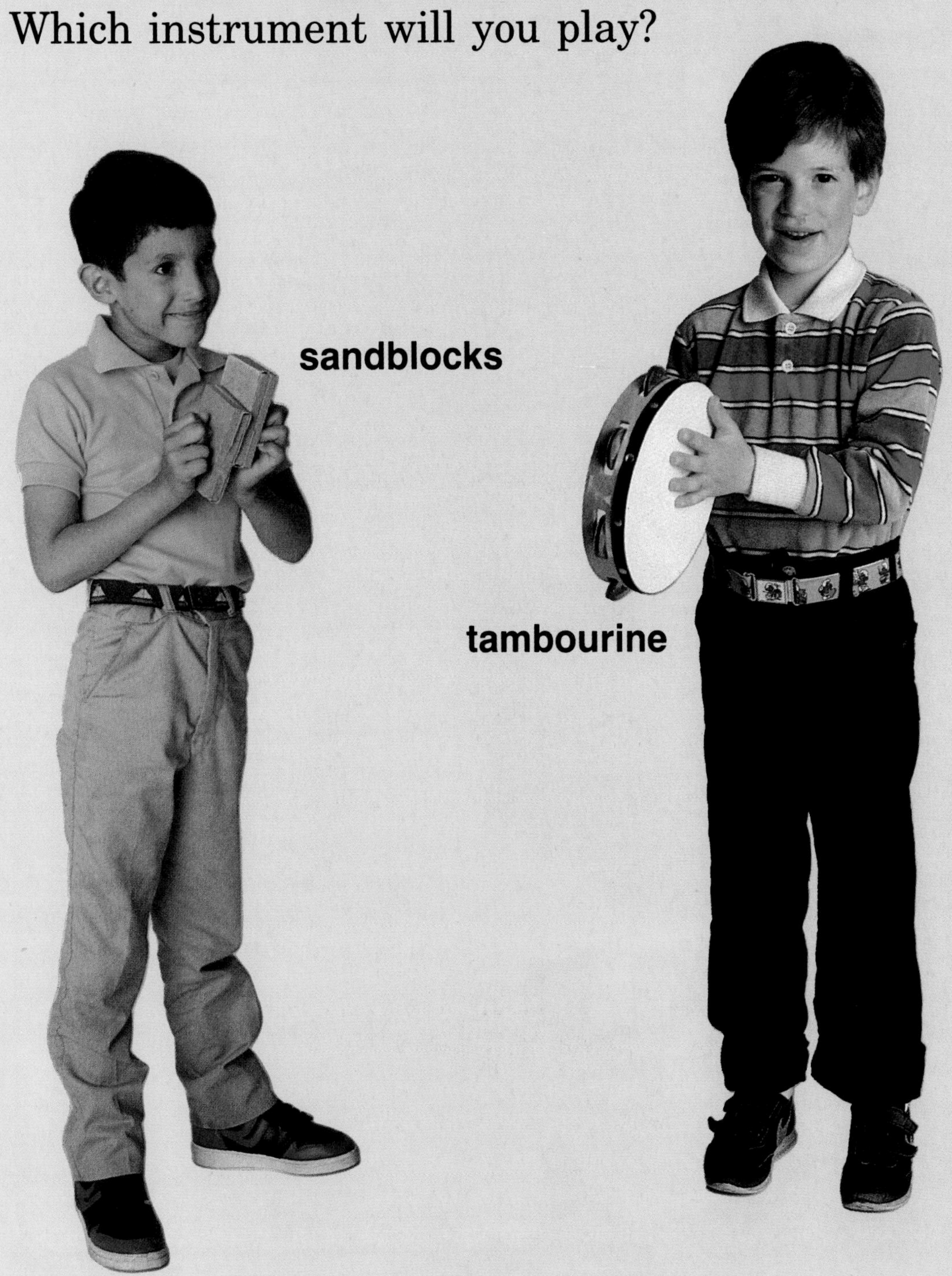
sandblocks
tambourine

maraca
jingle bells
bongos

A Marching Song

You can play a bell part with this song.
The notes will help you.

Noble Duke of York ④

Play-Party Game

4

1. Oh, the noble Duke of York,
   He had ten thousand men; He

B
C

led them up to the top of the hill, And he

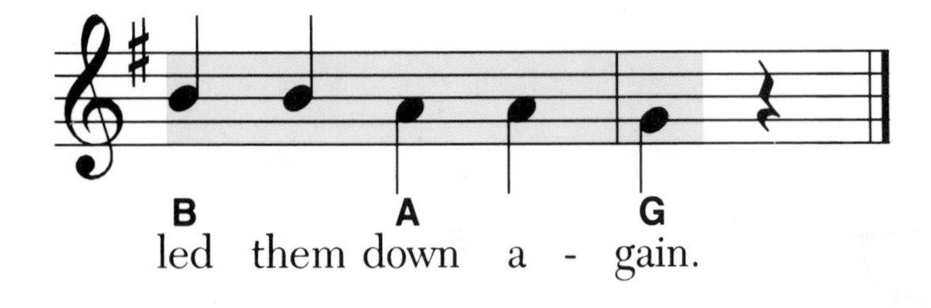
B
A
G

led them down a - gain.

2. Now, when we're up, we're up;
And when we're down, we're down; And
B
C
when we're on - ly half - way up, We're
B
A
G
nei - ther up nor down.

Marche Militaire

Listen to the recording.

Look at the pictures.

Can you tell which movement best fits the music?

LISTENING
4
SKILLS

<u>Marche militaire No. 1</u> (excerpt)
. . . . Schubert

N314BB

Sounds of Instruments

Listen for these instruments on the recording.

Which instrument do you hear first?

trumpet

drums

clarinet
trombone

A Nonsense Song

Listen for the story that this song tells.

There Was a Man

American Folk Tune   Words by Jeanne Wilhelms

1. In old - en days there was a man

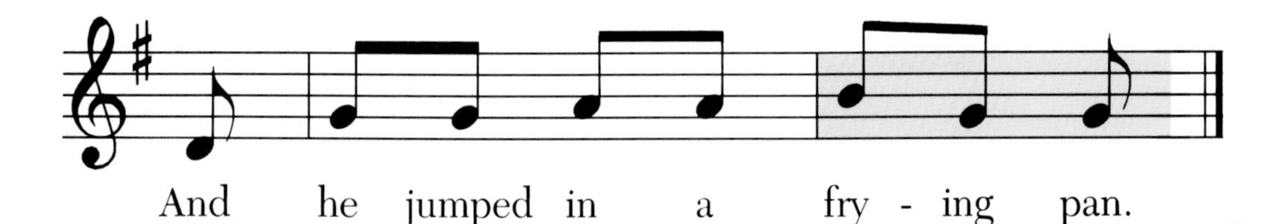
And he jumped in a fry - ing pan.

2. The frying pan it was so nice
And he jumped in a bag of ice.

ICE

3. The bag of ice it turned to slush
And he jumped in a pan of mush.

One More River

Look at the boxes below.
They show steady beats.

Play the F and C bells.
Rest if a box is empty.

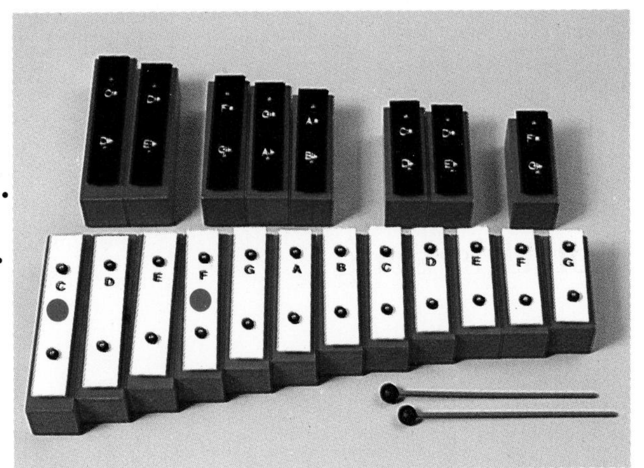

C
D
E
F
G
A
B
C
D
E
F
G

F		F	
One	more	river,	___ and
C		F	
that's the	river of	Jor -	dan;
F		F	
One	more	river,	_ There's
C		F	
one more	river to	cross.	______

Playing Bells

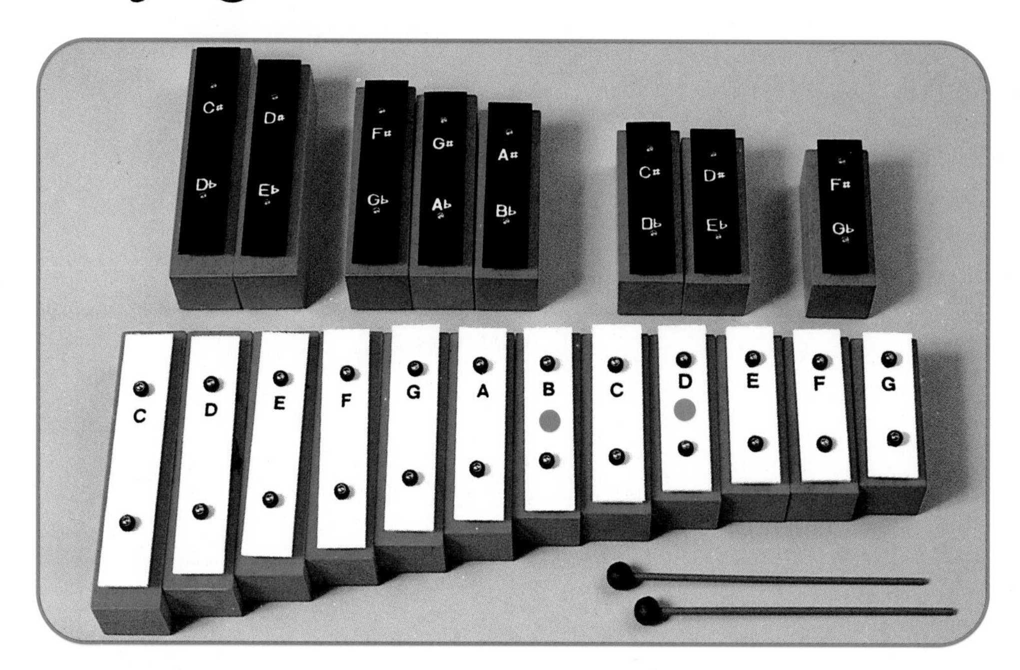
C♯
D♭
D♯
E♭
F♯
G♭
G♯
A♭
A♯
B♭
C♯
D♭
D♯
E♭
F♯
G♭
C
D
E
F
G
A
B
C
D
E
F
G

Here is a bell part for "All Night, All Day."

Which bells does the part use?

Practice the bell part.

Then play the bells as the class sings the song.

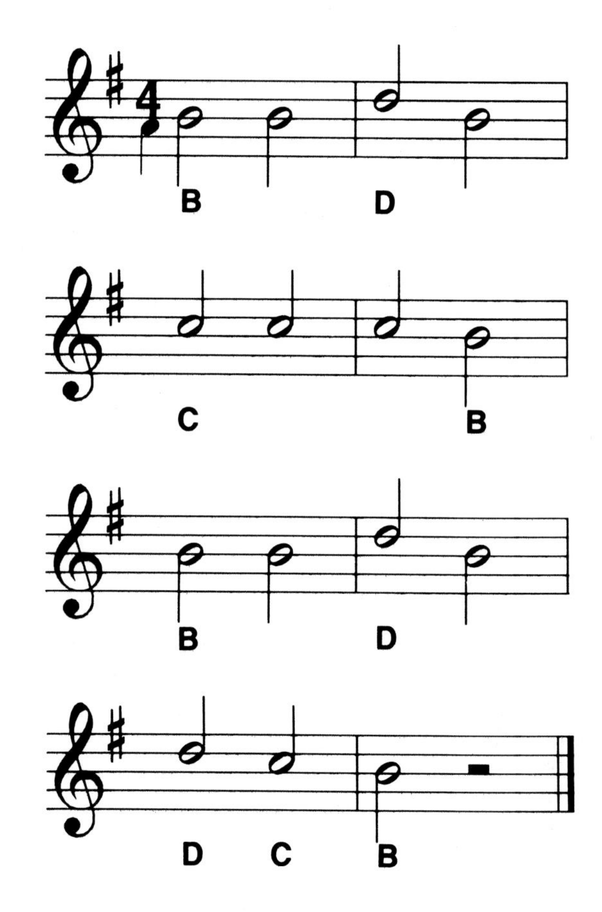
B
D
C
B
B
D
D
C
B

Playing Instruments

Look at the curved lines below.
They show the phrases in "Hi-dee-roon."

Play steady beats on the instrument pictured for each phrase.

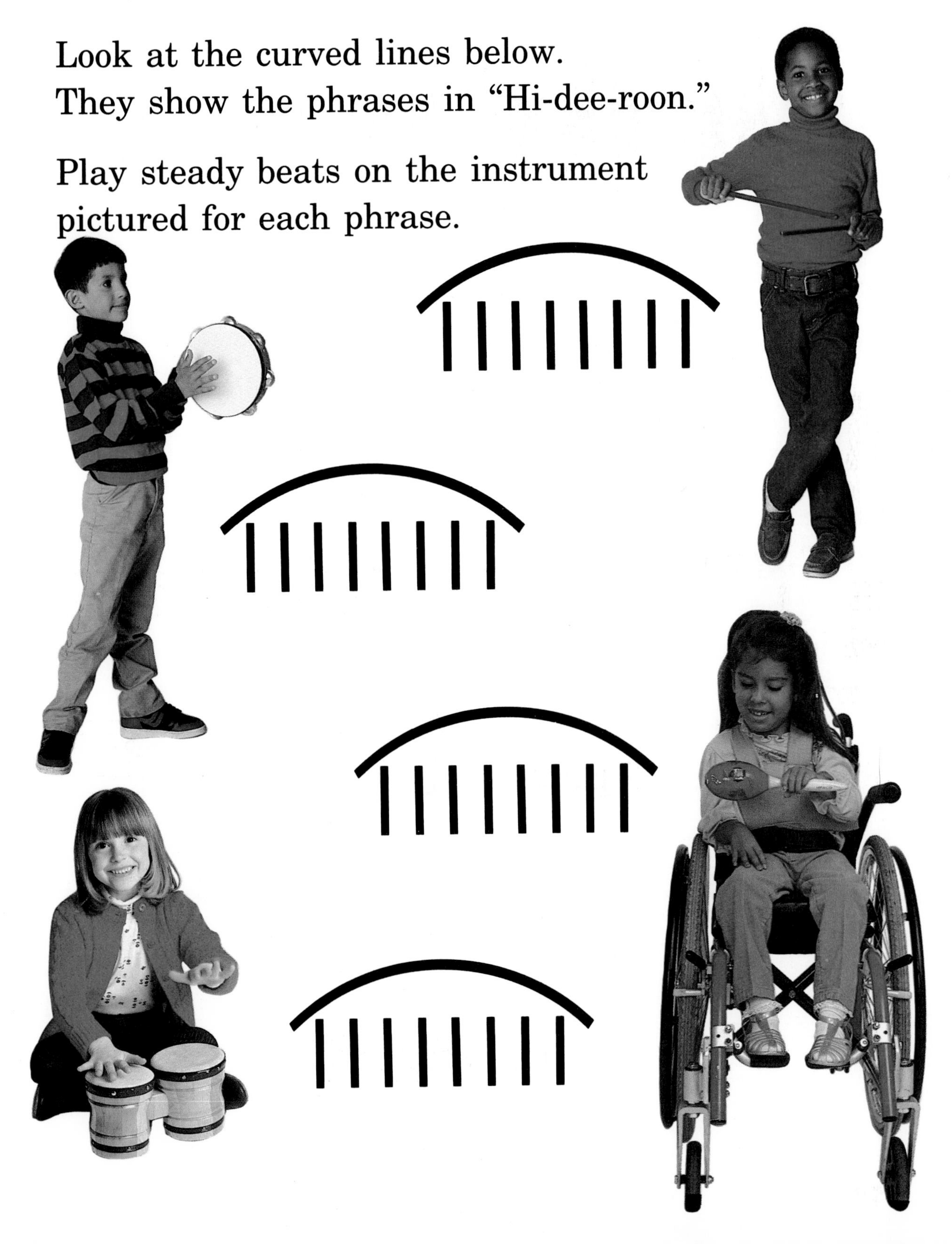

A Traditional Song

Help the singers on the recording spell Bingo's name.

Make the letters fit this pattern:

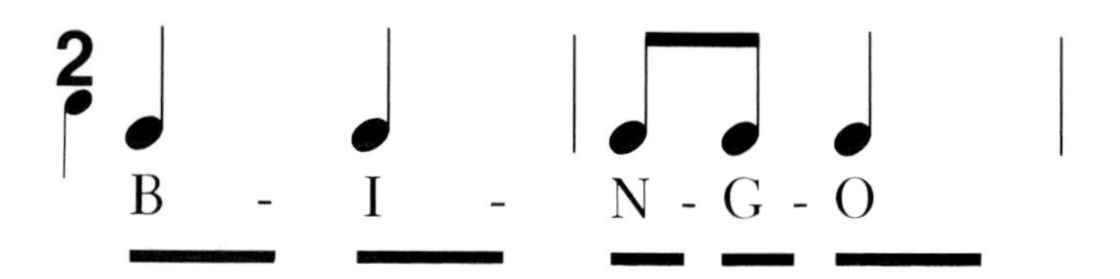
B - I - N - G - O

Bingo

American Folk Song

There was a farm - er had a dog,

And Bin - go was his name - o.

B - I - N - G - O,

B - I - N - G - O,

B - I - N - G - O,

And Bin - go was his name - o.

Rhythm-Pattern Detectives

Look at this rhythm pattern.

Its sound is long, long, short - short, long.
Can you find the pattern in the music?

Clap Your Hands 5

American Folk Song

A

Clap, clap, clap your hands,

Clap your hands to - geth - er.

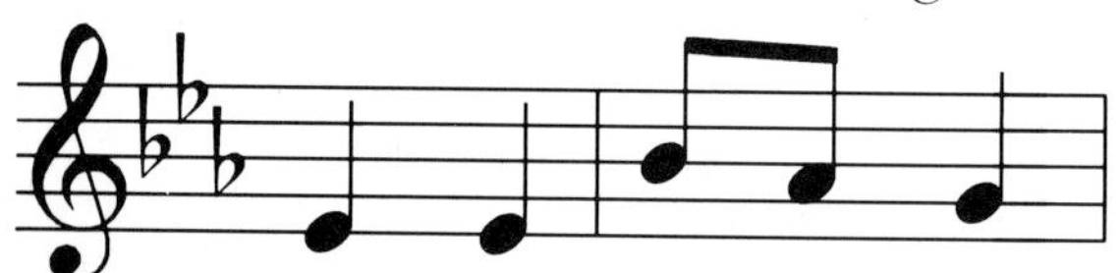

Clap, clap, clap your hands,

Clap your hands to - geth - er.

B

La la la la la la la,
La la la la la la,
La la la la la la la,
La la la la la la.

Playing Bells

Six Little Ducks

Folk Song from Maryland

1. Six little ducks that I once knew,
   Fat ones, skinny ones, fair ones, too,
   But the one little duck with a feather in his back,
   He led the others with a

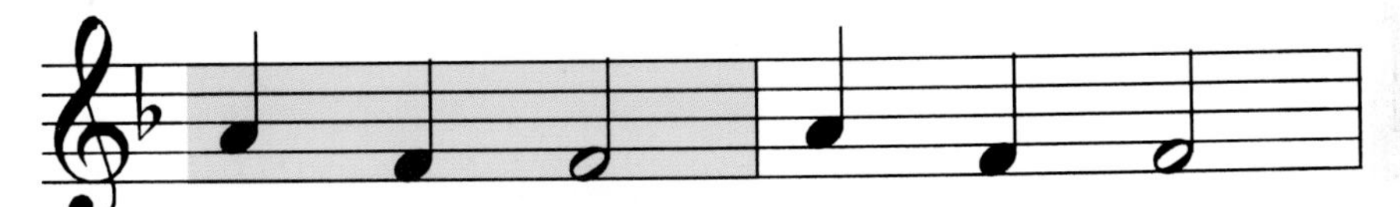

quack, quack, quack, quack, quack, quack;

He led the others with a

quack, quack, quack, quack, quack, quack.

2. Down to the river they would go,
   Wibble, wobble, wibble, wobble, to and fro, . . .
3. Home from the river they would come,
   Wibble, wobble, wibble, wobble, ho-hum-hum, . . .

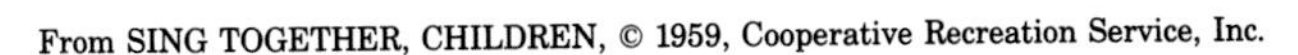

An Action Song

You can do actions
when you sing this song.

The pictures on the
next page will help you.

Under the Spreading Chestnut Tree

American Action Song

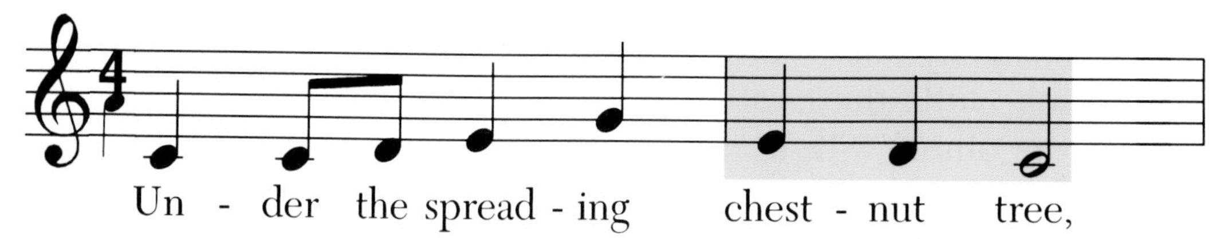
Un - der the spread - ing chest - nut tree,

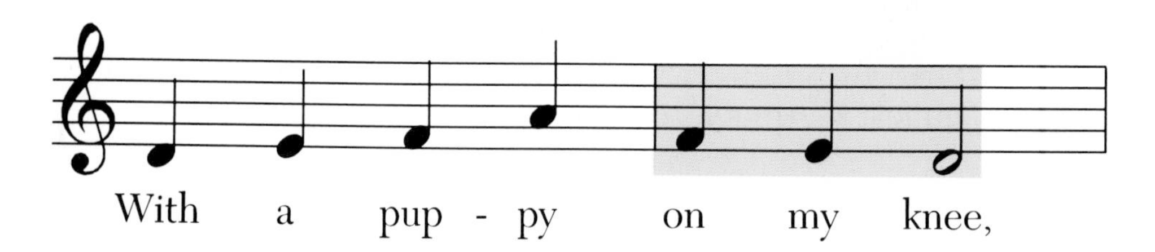
With a pup - py on my knee,

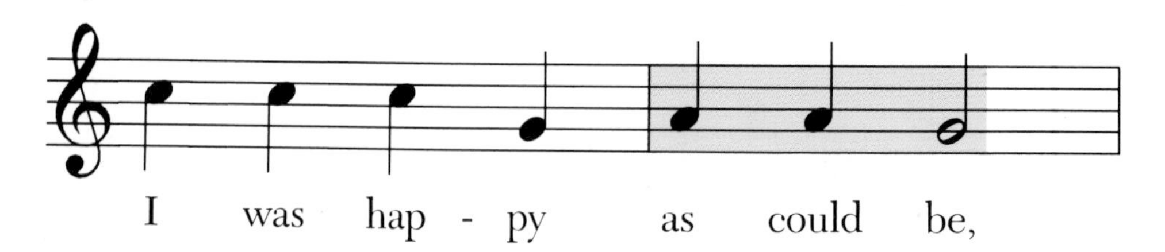
I was hap - py as could be,

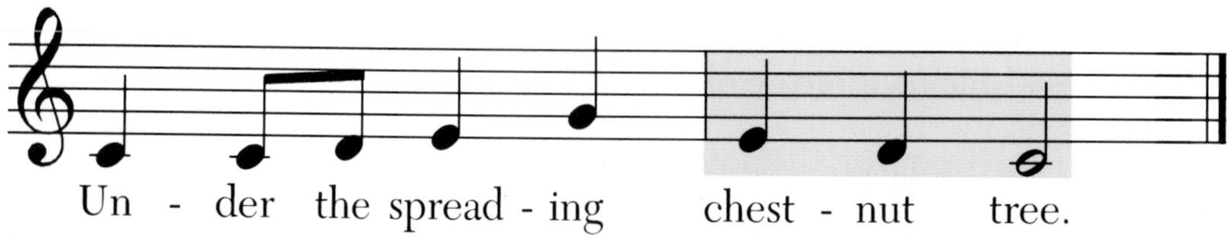
Un - der the spread - ing chest - nut tree.

Where do you see this rhythm pattern in the song?

♩ ♩ 𝅗𝅥

spreading
chest
- nut
tree
puppy
knee
happy

Gavotte

This is a line score.
It shows how sounds move.

Follow the score as you
listen to the music.

LISTENING
6
SKILLS

"Gavotte" from French Suite No. 5 in G Major . . . . Bach

Ⓐ

1.

2.

3.

4.

B

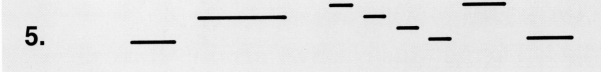

5.

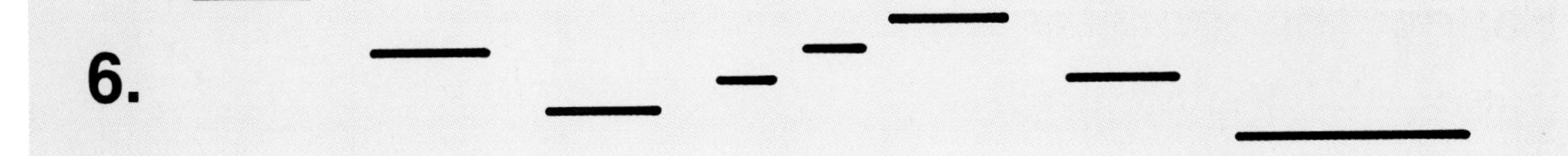

6.

7. ?

8.

9.

10.

11.

One Big Happy Family

—a Theme Musical by Carmino Ravosa

There are many kinds of families.
Who is in your family?

February

14

Can you play
I love you?

Sing and Celebrate

"Skinnamarink"
Valentine
Mailbox

Sounds of Halloween

What Halloween sounds do you hear in this song?

Halloween

Words and Music by Moiselle Renstrom

1. Oo, ________________________

'Tis the night of Hal - low - een;

Oo, ________________________

When such fun - ny things are seen.

Oo, ______________ Oo, ______________ BOO!

2. Oo, ______________________
Witches, black cats, goblins, too;
Oo, ______________________
All will try to frighten you.

I Know a Secret!

US MAIL

I've a Secret Valentine

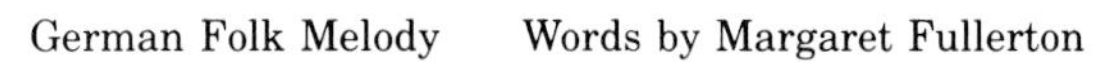
German Folk Melody Words by Margaret Fullerton

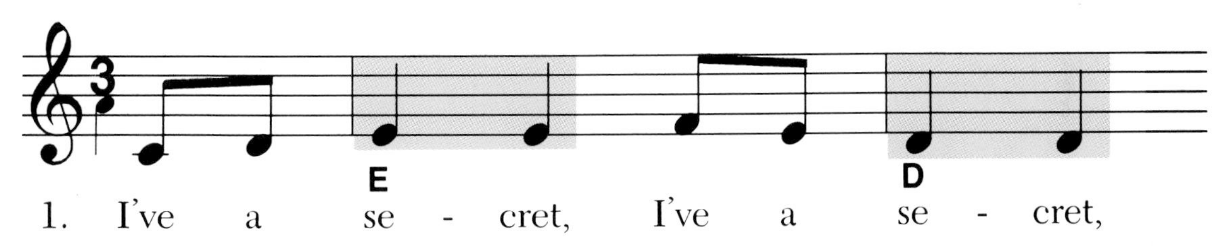
E
D
1. I've a se - cret, I've a se - cret,

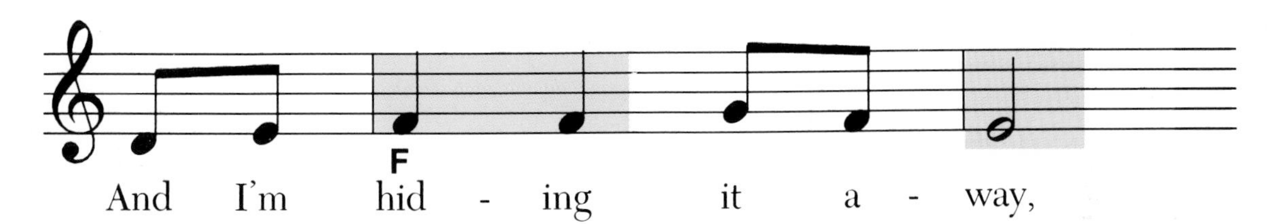
F
And I'm hid - ing it a - way,

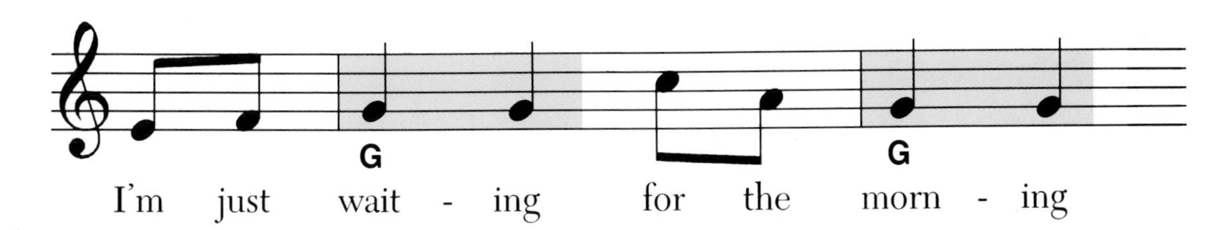
G
G
I'm just wait - ing for the morn - ing

Of Saint Val - en - tine's Day.

2. Oh, I hope you'll like my secret,
For I think it's very fine,
And it says I'm choosing someone
For my own Valentine.

Can You Read This?

You can read words.

I love you

You can read signs.

Now you can learn to read music.
These lines show steady beats:

▬ ▬ ▬ ▬

These sounds are shorter.
They are closer together.

▬▬ ▬▬ ▬▬ ▬▬

Here is a pattern to clap:

▬ ▬▬ ▬ ▬ | ▬ ▬ ▬▬

These notes show the same pattern:

This pattern is used in many songs.
Can you name another one?

Look for the same pattern here.
Where did you find it?

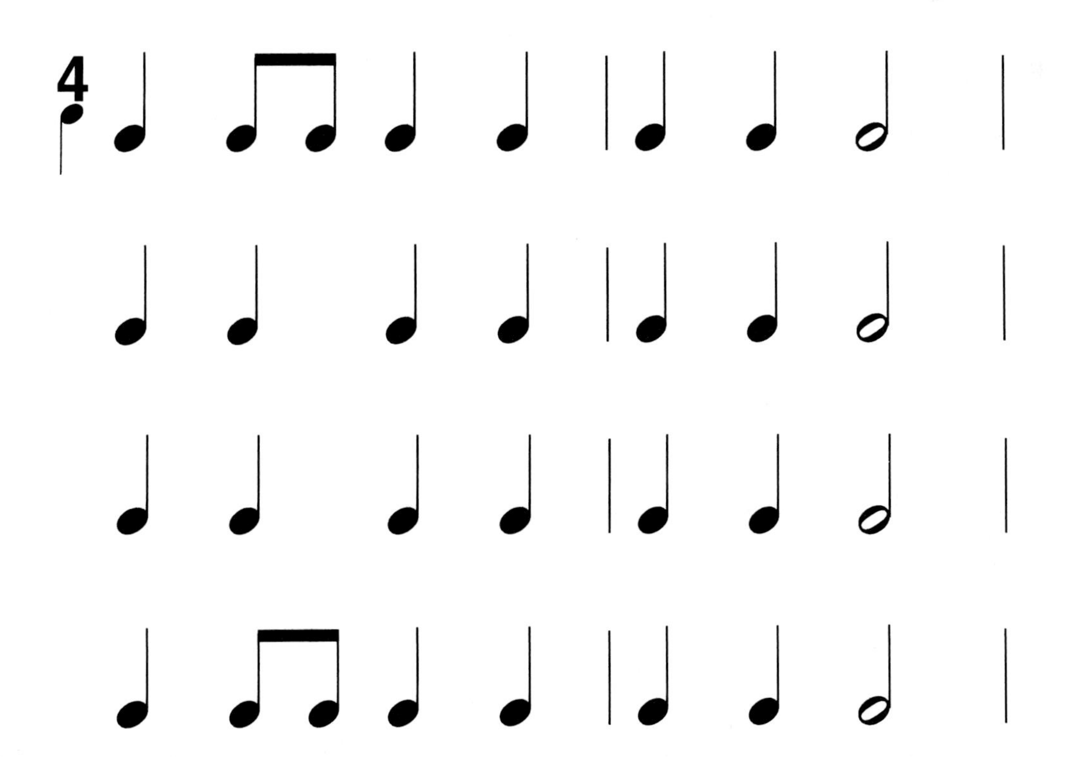

The Sound Bank

Classroom Instruments

How can you make sounds with these?

claves
rhythm sticks
gong
woodblock
tone block
tom-tom
cowbell
triangle
bongo
cymbal
finger cymbals
autoharp